I0476062

ECONOMIC MIND

Of

GOD

Peter Alexander Egom

Economic Mind of God

Published in Nigeria by

Adioné Publishing
The Equal Opportunity Publishers
Ukala Okpunor
Oshimili North LGA
Delta State, Nigeria
www.adione.net
e-mail: pub@adione.net

*Biblical references from the Good News Bible
Today's English Version*

ISBN 10 : 146 092 984 5
ISBN 13 : 978 - 146 092 984 1

Typeset in 11.5pt Book Antiqua by Jonas Nyarko
Printed in Nigeria by Printserve Limited

Contents

Illustrations

Dedication

To

Laerke, Magnus & Kasper,

my grandchildren

Preface

"Do not deceive yourselves, no one makes a fool of God. People will reap exactly what they sow. If they sow in the field of their natural desires, from it they will gather the harvest of death; if they sow in the field of the Spirit, from the Spirit they will gather the harvest of eternal life. So let us not become tired of doing good; for if we do not give up, the time will come when we will reap the harvest". Galatians 6:7-9

The Bible, stripped to the barest essentials of its ethical *langue* and its millennia of ethical *parole**, as Ferdinad de Saussure, 1857-1913, the pioneer Swiss structural linguist, would have said, is the Constitution of the Christian. Therefore, every inch and every second of the life of the Christian on this earth, from the cradle to the grave, must take its cue from, and defer to, the one aspect or the other of the *langue* and the *parole* of the Decalogue. This is what *Micah 6:8* says and means about the life of the Christian Kingdom-rider, who must always endeavour to take every thought captive in obedience to Christ; *2 Corinthians 10:5*.

Accordingly, there is nothing like a *secular* Christian society where Christians may live and act every inch and every second of their lives on this earth without taking their cues from, and paying due deference to, the one aspect or the other of the *langue* and the *parole* of the Decalogue. In other words, *ethical relativism* is not part of the transcendental ethical language of the Bible and this is what *Revelation/Apocalypse 3:15-16* tells us. Indeed, ethical relativism is the subtle, but very misleading, language of the materialistic faith and religion of Mammon. Thus, ethical relativism, by allowing the *mind-Christian* to indulge in the blasphemous bad manners of questioning the transcendental wisdom and benevolence of God, is the mind-Christian's first-class ticket to *Second Death* and eternal damnation.

The *langue* and the *parole* of the Decalogue contain the eternal and invariant ethical beacons of Kairos which God, the *Unchangeable Changer,* has set out to guide us Christians, the earthly Kingdom-riders, in our life-long earthly journey

---

* *Tradition* for Roman Catholics and *Sunnah* for Muslims

towards the Kingdom of God on this earth, and this paradise of God on earth is located precisely where Kairos, the abode of God, *intersects and overlaps* with Chronos, our current abode on earth. How then can we expect the ethical rules that are meant to guide us, the earthly Kingdom-riders, to God's Garden of Eden on this earth to be a *chameleon* of an affair, all depending on the whims and caprices of us mortals? No, ethical relativism is definitely the language of a created being that is trapped in Chronos, a being like Mammon himself!; it is certainly not part of the transcendental ethical charter for the life of a *true and heart-Christian.*

So, what this booklet: *Economic Mind of God,* tells any Christian is that *Trinitarian Economics* is the *Economic Constitution* of the Christian and that the economic life of any *heart-Christian* must take its cue from, and defer to, the *integrity principle* of currency market management in the Kingdom society, *Leviticus: 19:35-36, Deut; 25:13-14; Micah 6:10-11* and *Amos 8:5;* the *solidarity principle* of financial market management in the Kingdom society, *Psalm 15:5, Exodus 22:25, Luke 6:38, 2 Corinthians 8:13-15;* and the *subsidiarity principle* of commodity/industrial market management in the Kingdom society, *Deut. 32-8-9, Acts 17:26-27, 1 Peter 4:10, Matthew 25:14-30, Luke 19:11-27,* in order that the heart Christian may make it to the Kingdom of God on this earth; *Egom, 2007a, pp 177-257.* For, as *Galatians 6:7-8* says it, every inch and every second of the life of the heart-Christian on this earth involves, of necessity, a decision as to who to serve: God or Mammon?; *Joshua 24:15.*

No one should, then, ever be in any doubt at all that God has

His Own meticulous and win-win economic programme of justice, peace and development for man on this earth. For with *Genesis 47:13-26*, alone, we see how God provides humanity with the divine and evolutionary market master-plan for the past global rise, and the current global fall, of capitalism through the usury central banking ethic and practice of *1 Samuel 8:10-18* and *Nehemiah 9:36-37* and for the emerging financial rehabilitation of the globe to the justice and peace of His communitarian Kingdom of *live-and-let-live* on this earth by way of the *Balance Criterion* of the charity central banking ethic and practice of *Exodus 11:2-3, 12:35-36, 16:12-30, I Samuel 30:24* and *2 Corinthians 8:13-15*.

In fact, the world as we know it today is buckling under the increasing weight of the *money of inflation* of Mammon's law of usury and capitalism, see Fig. 1 below, and already, in the near horizon, we can see the clear outlines of the global economic restorative world and work of the *money of deflation* of God's law of charity and communitarianism, see Figs. 2 and 3 below. It is this emerging charity central banking ethic and practice of God which, by way of its restorative reticulation of capital from the surplus West to the deficit rest of the world through its exodus banks for regional and national settlements, will make citizens all and subjects none of each and everyone of us wherever we may find ourselves in the Kingdom society of this earth. *Marana tha!*

Peter Alexander Egom
Lagos, May 11, 2007

Acknowledgements

*T*his booklet, which introduces the contents of my new book: *"Economics of Justice & Peace"*, 2007a, is the edited and expanded text of my two-part lecture on *"Kingdom economic principles"* at the Full Gospel Business Men's Fellowship International, FGBMFI, S/W Ikoyi Chapter, Lagos, on April 26, 2007 and May 10, 2007.

I am exceedingly grateful to Mr. J.C. Obasi and the other members of this ecumenical Christian gathering for giving me the opportunity to flag off my life of economic evangelism on the platform of the FGBMFI. God will, no doubt, requite you abundantly on this score.

And the link-man who paved the way for my debut on the FGBMFI platform into economic evangelism is no other than my self-effacing friend, Moses Ohiomokhare, of Quintessence, Falomo, Lagos. Moses, may your sons be bishops!

About the Author

*P*eter Alexander Egom, a Nigerian, read social anthropology at Downing College, Cambridge, England, 1963 – 66 and national oekonomi at Aarhus University, Aarhus, Denmark, 1968 – 73.

He has, since 1974, researched and published works on the ethics of money and how this finds expression in varying national and global moneyflows, or central banking, systems. His recent published works are *"Globalization at the Crossroads: Capitalism or Communalism?"'* 2002; *"NEPAD and the Common Good"'* 2004; *"Compass for Economic Reform"*, 2006, *"Economics of Justice & Peace"* , 2007a, *"Economic Mind of God"*, 2007b.

Mr. Egom, essayist, economic theologian/evangelist and a Cambridge Full Blue in Athletics from 1966, lives in Lagos. He is the founding publisher of Adioné, *The Equal Opportunity Publishers,* www.adione.net, and, as well, the promoter/co-ordinator of ACCOSCO: *African Capital & Commodity Services Company,* www.accosco.net, the pan-African human capital and market development initiative for growing intra-African trade, payments and investment flows.

Theory

"And now we are slaves in the land that you gave us, this fertile land which gives us food. What the land produces goes to the kings that you put over us because we sinned. They do as they please with us and our lifestock and we are in deep distress"

Nehemiah 9:36-37.

1   Nature of Economics

1.1   Economics is a moral science. It draws public attention to the various types and structures of the market and power relations that emerge between and among persons, in any money economy of the globe, as either the top-to-bottom and *might-is-right* social ethic of Mammon or the bottom-to-top and *right-is-might* social ethic of God becomes the organizing market rule and spiritual anchor of their everyday decisions on what to produce, how and for whom; *Egom, 2004, pp 54 - 56*. Economics educates us, therefore, on how to use either Mammon's public-sector debt concept of money or God's private sector commodity concept of money to organize the uneven or the even distribution, respectively , of work and its rewards, social and material, among and between people of sex, age, creed and race in any society of the globe.

1.2   Whereas fiscalist or capitalist economics educates us on how to use Mammon's public sector debt concept of money to organize the uneven and hierarchic distribution of work and its rewards across the age, sex, race, creed, etc. divides of society, monetarist or communitarian economics educates us on how to use God's private sector commodity concept of money to organize the even and leveling distribution of work and its rewards among and between people of sex, age, race, creed, etc. in any society of the globe. Thus, any theory and practice of economic life in any society of the globe, past, present and future, must be hinged on, held together and driven by either the capitalist, discriminatory and non-solidary public sector debt money or by the communitarian, non-discriminatory and solidary private sector commodity money; *Egom, 2007a, pp. 3-50.*

1.3 When interest-based public sector debt money is the driver of economic policy in any society of the globe, then the uneven-playing economic field of market monopoly/monopsony and oligopoly/oligopsony, of hills and valleys, must emerge and remain between and among people in society after the unequal and apartheid economic mind of Mammon; *I Samuel 8:10-18, Nehemiah 9:36-37.* But, when the interest-free private sector commodity money drives economic policy in any society of the globe, then the even-playing economic field of market polypoly/polypsony emerges and remains among and between people of sex, creed, race, etc. after the equal and solidary Economic Mind of God; *Isaiah 32:1-4, 15-18.*

1.4 The nature of economics as a moral science is made clear by the fact that it is the choice a society makes on the type of money it should use to drive its economic policy which either makes citizens all and subjects none, or makes citizens few and subjects many, of its members. So, a society, by choosing the interest-based public sector debt money to drive its economic policy does, indeed, make a clear pitch for the *economics of social exclusion,* of citizens few and subjects many, after the avaricious and apartheid economic mind of Mammon. But, when a society chooses the interest-free private sector commodity money to drive its economic policy, it works, as of necessity, the *economics of social inclusion,* of citizens all and subjects none, after the sacrificial and solidary Economic Mind of God. Thus, interest-based money makes *people work for it,* where interest free-money *works for people.* Hence, as the saying goes, the former is a *bad master,* where the latter is a *good servant.*

2. Anatomy of Money

2.1   Money of any sort is a social relational, a political and an ethical cum spiritual phenomenon. For where two, three or more persons are gathered for market exchanges in the Spirit and Name of God, there must we find the interest-free private sector commodity money as the economic medium for weaving solidary and equal market relations between and among persons of creed, sex and race in any society of the globe. But where two, three or more persons are gathered for market exchanges in the spirit and name of Mammon, there do we find the interest-based public sector debt money as the medium of exchange which weaves apartheid and hierarchic market relations between and among persons of race, creed and sex in any society on this earth. In effect, the usury money of Mammon divides men unequally on the basis of race, gender and creed in the distribution of work and its rewards in society, but the charity money of God unites men equally, without any bias of gender, creed or race, in the distribution of work and its rewards in society; *Egom, 2007a, passim.*

2.2 The inequality of access to the economic opportunities of goods, services and jobs which the usury money of Mammon gives to people of race, gender and creed in any fiscalist or capitalist society, where interest-based public sector debt money is the driver of economic policy, has the following structural implications on how the currency, financial and commodity/industrial markets of such a society are organized; *Egom, 2004, pp 57 - 63.*

2.2.1 In its currency market, where its money of account, contracts and payments is produced for onward delivery into its financial and industrial/ commodity markets, we find that it is the deficit-financing public sector of society, and its coterie of the few private sector deficit-financing banks, that control the production and distribution of interest-based public sector debt money for society. So, in a fiscalist or capitalist society, one has access to new money and to effective demand only when one is grafted on to the patronage system of the officials of the public sector in Abuja, Nigeria, or in any other fiscal centre of global capitalist governance. This is the demand-led, top-to-bottom and consumption-prone method of money creation and distribution in society which is not production-friendly, people-friendly and rural-friendly. It is the money creation engine of the Okada, *motor-bike taxi,* and urban-friendly economy of citizens few and subjects many. This is, indeed, the *money of inflation* currency market of Mammon as one has it in Nigeria and elsewhere in the developing and non-convertible and, also, in the developed and financial convertible, currency capitalist world; *Egom, 2006, passim.*

2.2.2   In its market for savings, or financial market, it is the consumption-prone and deficit-financing public sector that is the destination of the bulk of the savings of society. Consequently, the instruments for savings mobilization and distribution in society become preponderantly short-term and risk-averting. Such a short-term savings market does not encourage the growth of the local content of jobs, goods and services in society, rather, it encourages the import of everything that could otherwise have been produced at home; *Egom, 2006, passim.* This is how the financial market of a fiscalist/capitalist economy encourages industrial outsourcing to the detriment of the home production and supply of the economic opportunities of goods, services and jobs.

2.2.3   Its market for commodities, or industrial market, is urban-friendly with the result there is always a headlong rush of men, materials and money from the rural areas to the urban areas. Such an industrial location policy engenders the loss of agricultural production in the rural areas of society as it provides for the massive import of food to make up for the endemic short-fall in home food production. In effect, the urban industrialisation model which the apartheid and usury money of Mammon supports in society is the enemy of job, food and social security for all in any fiscalist or capitalist society of the globe; *Egom, 2006, passim.*

2.3   However, the equality of access to the economic opportunities of goods, services and jobs which the charity money of God gives to people of race, gender and creed in any monetarist or communitarian society of the common good, where interest-free private sector commodity money drives economic policy, has the following structural consequences on how the currency, financial and commodity/industrial markets of such a society are organized; *Egom, 2004, pp 57-63*

2.3.1 In its currency market, we find that it is the legion of its rural private sector SMEs and cottage entrepreneurs, with their investment and commodity banking principals/sponsors, that control the production and distribution of interest-free private sector commodity money for society. Hence, in a monetarist or communitarian society one has access to new money and effective demand for the simple reason that one is, *first,* a human being with the birthright to the citizen wage, *Egom, 2004, pp 25-26,* and is, *second,* an entrepreneur who has a socially-approved and bankable cottage business proposal. This is the supply-leading, bottom-to-top and production-prone method of money creation and distribution in society which is local-content friendly, people-friendly and environment/rural friendly. It is the money creation and supply engine of the common good and rural-friendly economy of citizens all and subjects none. And it is, therefore, the *money of deflation* currency market of God as one found it in Joseph's Egypt of *Genesis 47:23-24* and will find it in every Kingdom national economy of the emerging global economy of communitarianism; *Egom, 2006, 2007a, passim.*

2.3.2   In its market for savings, or financial market, it is the production-prone and self-financing private sector cottage entrepreneur that is the main destination of the savings of society. Consequently, the instruments for savings mobilisation and distribution in society become largely medium-to-long-term and risk-taking. Such a medium-long-term savings market is the ruralised grower of the local content of jobs, goods and services in society. This is how the financial market of a monetarist or communitarian economy encourages industrial in-sourcing and self-reliance and ensures, thereby, the presence of job, food and social security for all in society; *Egom, 2006, 2007a, passim.*

2.3.3   In its market for commodities, or industrial market, local resources are used largely for the satisfaction of local needs so that emphasis is placed on the minimization of transportation costs in the sourcing of jobs, goods and services. Such an industrial location policy engenders the plentiful production of local food varieties in society with the result that food security is assured for all in society. In effect, the rural industrialisation model which the charity and solidary money of God supports in society is the source and sustainer of job, food and social security for all in any monetarist or communitarian society of the emerging economic Kingdom of God on this earth; *Egom, 2006, 2007a, passim.*

2.4   So, in the light of above, money of any sort is a social-relational, a political and an ethical sum spiritual phenomenon for three market-related reasons as follows; *Egom, 2006, pp 29-60, Egom, 2007a, pp. 3-50.* One, in the currency market of any society it specifies who and who should control the production of its unit of account, contracts and payments and distribute such into society's financial circulation of money and industrial circulation of money as well. Accordingly, we find that where the apartheid and usury money of Mammon concentrates the control of society's currency market in the hands of the public sector- related and urban-based private banking few, the solidary and charity money of God disperses the control of society's currency market in the hands of its many rural and bi-cameral micro-finance banks, MFBs. Two, in the financial market of any society, it indicates who and who should be the preferred end-users and destinations of the bulk of society's savings. Thus it is that where public sector debt money uses the bulk of society's savings to finance the deficits of the consumption-prone and urban-based public sector, private sector commodity money uses the bulk of society's savings to finance the seed, working and growth capital of the many rural cottage entrepreneurs and SMEs. And three, in the commodity/industrial market of any society, it indicates how work and the social and material rewards of work should be organized and distributed among men on the ground, or spatially. Hence, where the apartheid money of Mammon emphasizes the rural-urban drift of labour, capital and materials in the service of the conspicuous consumption of foreign content by the urban and public-sector-controlling private few, solidary money of God insists on the reversal of the rural-urban drift of labour, capital and materials in the service of growth in the local content of job, food and social security for each and all in society. In effect, where public sector debt money charts the apartheid and hierarchic urban industrialisation roadmap for the current kingdom of Mammon on earth, private sector commodity money splays out the solidary and subsidiary rural industrialisation roadmap for the emerging Kingdom of God on this earth; *www.globaljusticemovement.com*

3. Economics is Central Banking

3.1 The use of money of any sort to organize the distribution of work and its rewards, social and material, among and between people of sex, race and creed in any society occurs through money-based activities in the currency, financial and industrial / commodity markets of society. So, money of any sort generates a triple moneyflows market structure in any society of the globe and this is why the moral science of economics is all about managing the moneyflows market structure of any society either in the service of the few and at the expense of the many or in the service of all and at the expense of none. And this is preciselywhat the moral science of central banking is all about. For, **economics is central banking;** *Adione-Egom, 2002, pp 46 - 65, Egom 2004, pp 121 - 185; Egom, 2007a, pp. 115-173.* And, because public sector debt money is to the apartheid and capitalist economics of Mammon what private sector commodity money is to the solidary and communitarian economics of God, it follows that public sector debt money is to the usury central banking ethic of Mammon, what private sector commodity money is to the charity central banking ethic of God.

3.2 The usury central banking ethic of Mammon ordains a top-to-bottom moneyflows market structure for any society as one finds it in *1 Samuel 8:10   18. Nehemiah 9:36-37.* Herein, the public sector -related private and urban few in society consume without working and thereby entrench the urban industrialisation roadmap into the socio-economic fabric of society. It is this central banking ethic of the survival of the fittest that engenders the live-and-let-die and explosively urbanized Okada-*motor bike taxi*-economies of the modern day as one finds them in Nigeria, Democratic Republic of the Congo, Kenya, South Africa, etc. In these economies, money is created by the few for the few in the true diabolical spirit of the Structural Adjustment Programmes of the IMF and the World Bank. It is, thus, that the usury central banking ethic of Mammon makes citizens few and subjects many of the members of any capitalist society of the centre and of the periphery.

3.3   In contrast to the above, the charity central banking ethic of God engenders a bottom-to-top moneyflows market structure in the economic life of society as one finds it in *Genesis 41:48-49* and *Genesis 47:23-24.* Herein, the private sector rural many produce society into such social and material plenty that the live-and-let-live canopy of justice and peace envelops society as we find it in *Judges 18:7, Isaiah 32:15-18.* and *Ezekiel 38:12.* What happens, therefore, in any society that works the charity central banking ethic of God is that solidary private sector commodity money welds society's financial and industrial markets into an enduring feast of sustained and exponential growth in the local content of jobs, goods and services. It is, in this way, that the emerging Kingdom of God on this earth will make citizens all and subjects none of us in Nigeria and, likewise, of all in any other society of this earth.

4.   Trinitarian Economics

4.1   When the currency market of any society is controlled by the consumption-prone public sector and its coterie of deficit-financing banks, what we get is an interest-based unit of account, contracts and payments in society which is *short-of-breath* in society's currency and financial markets and, is, therefore, indifferent to growing the local content of jobs, goods and services in society's industrial / commodity market. This is the true character of the *money of inflation* which emerges and remains in any society where the consumption-prone public sector is in charge of its currency market. And, this is what *inflation-targeting* monetary policy brings about in any society; *Egom, 2006, p. 173.* Value integrity is simply sapped from the unit commodity value of society's currency through the unbridled production of money from the *thin air* to finance the unbridled consumption binges of the few public sector overlords and their accompanying palace touts. So, the regime of indirect-financing of the usury central banking ethic of Mammon is the enemy of growth in the local content of jobs, goods and services.

4.2   But, when the currency market of any society is controlled by the production-prone SME private sector and its legion of rural investment and commodity banking sponsors, what we get is an interest-free unit of account, contracts and payments in society which is *full-of-breath* in society's currency and financial markets and, is therefore, very *gung-ho* about growing the local content of jobs, goods and services in society's industrial / commodity market. This is the true character of the *money of deflation* which emerges and remains in any society where the production-prone SME private sector is in charge of its currency market. And this is what *deflation-targeting* monetary policy brings about in any society; *Egom, 2006, pp. 57-58.* The currency of society is endowed with unit-commodity-value integrity for the simple reason that money creation and distribution in society is channeled directly from its currency and financial markets, *without any inflationary leakages*, into society's commodity / industrial market for the production of the local content of jobs, goods and services. And this is the true manner of work of the charity central banking ethic of God in any society of the globe. The supply of inflation-free and interest-free money in society's currency and financial markets creates its own demand for the local content of jobs, goods and services in society's industrial / commodity market. Thus it is that the regime of direct-financing in society is the promoter of its growth in local content.

4.3   *"What he requires of us is this: to do what is just, to show constant love, and to live in humble fellowship with our God", Micah 6:8.* How, then, does this triple set of what God demands of each of us in society fit into the practice of the charity central baking ethic of God? This is precisely the concern of Trinitarian Economics as follows; *Egom, 2007a, pp. 177-257.*

4.3.1 We know from *Leviticus 19:35-36, Deut 25:13-14, Micah 6:10-11* and *Amos 8:5* that God does not like us to cheat with economic weights and measures in the market places of society. So the currency market management principle of Trinitarian economics demands that the unit-commodity-value of a currency in society's currency market is always full and constant. It is such a currency of unit commodity value integrity that is the foundation for the level-playing market field that enables Tom, Dick and Harry in society to be mobilized into emptying themselves of their innate talents in the service of all to the glory of God. This is the métier of private sector commodity money as we see it at work in the Pharaoh's Egypt of *Genesis 47:23-26*. In effect, there is distributive justice in a Trinitarian economy because its currency is created to have unit commodity value integrity and, thus, an invariant purchasing power yesterday, today and forever in the, *semper idem: always the same*, mould of God the Father.

4.3.2   If we must empower each human being of creed, sex and race in society in his own individual enterprise of calling, in his own cultural and native environment, then the Trinitarian economy must have a savings structure which is mobile, sacrificial and entrepreneur-friendly. This type of financial market arises, as of logical necessity, in any society whose currency market creates and distributes a currency with a full and constant unit commodity value. Hence, such a patient and long-suffering savings market can only exist when and where there is the interest-free regime of direct financing in society as demanded of us in *Psalm 15:5* and *Exodus 22:25*. In fact, such a sacrificial and solidary savings structure which goes out to every rural nook and cranny of society to stoke up the entrepreneurship of people of race, creed and sex encapsulates the interest-free *Mine is Thine* savings mobilisation and distribution ethic of the *Nazareth Manifesto* of our

Lord and Saviour Jesus Christ, *Luke 4:18-19*. So, the direct and equity financing ethos of the Trinitarian economy is in the best savings management tradition of God the Son of showing constant and sacrificial love as in *Luke 6:38, 19:1-27, 2 Corinthians 8:13-15*.

4.3.3   The production structure of the Trinitarian economy is a web of rural or cottage entrepreneurs who are empowered to remain and work where God has assigned them to be on this earth as we find it in *Deut. 32:8-9* and *Acts 17:26-27*, and to use the resources locally available to them to feed, and create jobs for, themselves and for others to the glory of God. This is what gives rise to the industrial subsidiarity and the climate for entrepreneurship that is talked about and encouraged for all Christians in *1 Peter 4:10, Luke 19:11-27* and *Matthew 25:14-30*.   And, this is the industrial ruralisation roadmap which the charity central banking ethic of God fosters in the emerging Trinitarian economies of the globe. In   these economies every human being is given the opportunity to stand out and be counted in work and in reward and to, thus, live in humble stewardship and fellowship with God, *as the Holy Spirit directs.*

In effect, as the charity central banking ethic of God imposes the currency value integrity market rule on the currency market of society, so does it *derivatively* impose the savings equitisation and solidarity market rule on its financial market and the industrial ruralisation, subsidiarity and entrepreneurship market rule on its industrial /

commodity market. It is in this way that Trinitarian economics enables each and everyone of us to always *"do what is just, to show constant love and to live in humble fellowship with our God"*. For, integrity is the just and even-handed attribute of God the Father, solidarity is the merciful and sacrificial attribute of God the Son and subsidiarity is the energising and entrepreneurial attribute of God the Holy Spirit.

4.4   Christians know from Exodus 20:2-6, Deut. 5:6-10; 6:4-5, that only *One God*, and no other god, should be worshipped.   They also know from John 14:10-11; 15:26; 16:17, that there are *Three Persons* in *One God*: God the Father: *The Creator*: God the Son: *The Redeemer*, and God the Holy Spirit: *The Sanctifier*. So, Christians distinguish between the Three Persons of One God by the *works* they perform, the *activities* they do. Accordingly, Trinitarian Economics educates us on how the Three Persons of One God go to work in managing the respective currency, financial and industrial/commodity markets of any economy *as God desires it*. However, this Doctrine of the Holy Trinity, which is the bedrock of the Christian Faith, is not acceptable to mind-Christians and to non-Christians as well. Why is this so? Because mind-Christians and non-Christians, alike, want to comprehend the Mind of God and His world of Kairos with the aid of their puny created minds! *An impossibility; Isaiah 55:8-9*. Man is yet to make complete sense of his own created world of Chronos and how much less is he in the position to make any sense of Kairos, the world of his Creator and

Sustainer? Kairos is the abode of the Holy Trinity. It is a world of *mystery* and a no-go area for the human mind. *It is, thus, the world of unwavering* **faith** *in the word of God; Romans 1:17.* So, with regard to the *mystery of the Holy Trinity*, mind-Christians and non-Christians, alike, should heed what Ludwig Wittgenstein, the Austrian linguistic philosopher, says to those minds which are set on plumbing the depths of the mystery world of Kairos: *whereof one cannot speak, thereof one must be silent-***wovon mann nicht sprechen kann, daruber muss mann schwegen***

4.5   Trinitarian Economics, it must be emphasized, is not alone in forswearing the necessity of the twin fiscalist phenomena of Public Sector Borrowing Requirement, PSBR, and Interest for the common good of the peoples of any society of the globe. *Classical Economics*, *Binary Economics* and *Islamic Economics* do likewise; *Adione-Egom, 2002, Egom 2004, passim, www.globaljusticemovement.com.* All of these brands of interest-free economic thought and practice posit the necessity for a *Catholic* marriage between the money supply market structure /financial circulation of money and the money demand and use market structure/industrial circulation of money of any economy before it can begin to provide its members with job, food and social security. However, Trinitarian Economics distinguishes itself from its interest-free siblings in two specific ways as follows. First, it is categorical in saying that any economy of the globe is capable of making citizens all and subjects none of its members when and only when there is value integrity in its currency market, value solidarity in its financial market and value subsidiarity in its industrial/commodity market., And, second, it says, with emphasis, that the money supply market structure and the money demand and use market structure of any economy fuse to produce its members into social and material plenty only when *deflation-targeting* monetary policy has equipped the economy with a country-wide network of back-to-back stock and commodity exchanges as in Genesis 41:48-49. In other words, Trinitarian Economics tells us that a market economy makes citizens all and subjects none of its members only when its overall market structure for currencies, savings, goods, services and ideas is supported by the *troika* of the currency market pillar of value integrity, the financial market pillar of value solidarity and the industrial/commodity market pillar of value subsidiarity. Can economic theory and practice be more elementary and more specific than this? Very unlikely! And it is this simple because the Holy Trinity is at work in promoting the market development and management of the common good economy of citizens all and subjects none after the *Economic Mind of God!*

Practice

"The wealthy cheat and rob. They ill-treat the poor and take advantage of foreigners. I looked for someone who could build a wall, who could stand in the places where the walls have crumbled and defend the land when my anger is about to destroy it, but I could find no one. So I will turn my anger loose on them and like a fire I will destroy them for what they have done" Ezekiel 22:29-31.

5. Biblical Model of Human Development

5.1   Most scholars of the Bible, and Christians in general, are sadly but sincerely unaware that the Books of the Bible, from *Genesis to Revelation/Apocalypse,* tell an incomparable story of development economics, both in theory and in practice However, one cannot say that this is what obtains with many economists of repute. For many an economist of renown of the past and the present has, in the one way or the other, borrowed, often without giving due credit to God, the one idea or the other from the divine and evolutionary economic programme of God as is contained in the Books of the Bible. This prophetic economic programme of the Bible, which has served as the theoretical launch-pad for many household names in economics, has three successive stages. From the barter economics of reciprocity and communalism *(Genesis to Ruth)* one moves to the money economics of usury and capitalism *(1 Samuel through Malachi to 2 Maccabees)* and, finally, one moves to the money economics of charity and communitarianism *(Matthew to Revelation /Apocalypse).*

5.2   It is this biblical and evolutionary market-master-plan of God for the development of the global economy into the steady social and material plenty of the communitarian economic Kingdom of God on earth that Karl Marx borrowed and transformed into the backbone of his evolutionary, but secular, three-stage theory of the market development of the global economy from the *rough- and-tumble grass* of communalism to the *utopian grace* of socialism and communism; *Egom 1977, passim*. In Marx's schema , one sees the global economy moving from the barter and agrarian sleepiness of distributive communalism into the interest-laced monetary strife and mayhem of distributive capitalism, both commercial and industrial, and finally into the interest-free, but *incongruously top-to-bottom,?,* monetary harmony and bliss of distributive socialism and communism; *Egom, 2007a, pp. 53-111*. In like manner, W.W. Rostow's stage theory of economic growth, 1960, *"The Stages of Economic Growth: A Non-Communist Manifesto"*, is a major example, among other pro-capitalist works, of an evolutionary economic programme that leans heavily on the economic programme of God without ever having the decency of saying so. Besides, Rostow, like Francis Fukuyama, long after him in 1992: *"The End of History and the Last Man"*, truncates the evolutionary economic programme of the Bible at the stage of the money economics of usury and capitalism, and, thereby, condemns the globe to the eternal reign of the euro-centric economics of apartheid. For capitalism is the global regime of political and economic apartheid, whose financial powerhouse is the reserve currency world of the West. And, even the UNDP endorses this idea that capitalism is the last stage in the evolutionary development of the global economy; *Egom, 2004, pp 149-150*. For its Human Development Index, HDI, is a *backward-looking and classificatory model* of how apartheid and usury money is being used to organize work and its rewards rather unevenly among and between persons and nations on the globe. The HDI is not a *forward-looking and transformational model* of how communitarian and charity money could and will be used to organize work and its rewards evenly among and between persons and nations in the global economy. This is to say that the HDI only classifies dying and dead persons and nations but does not tell us how and why those persons and nations are dead and are dying. Thus, whereas communitarian and charity money nudges the global economy towards a future of distributive justice and peace, apartheid and usury money entraps the global economy in the current entropic and bogus *war on terrorism* and in the current bogus and entropic *clash of civilizations.* For, let us face it, Islam and Christianity, because both subscribe to variants of the same interest-free economic agenda of the charity central banking ethic of God as indicated in 4.5 above, should not and do not have any ethical, political and economic problems with each other but do both have irreconcilable ethical, economic and political problems with capitalism, the materialistic, God-hating-and-baiting faith and religion of Mammon; *Egom, 2004, passim*

5.3   But how does one begin to decode the three-stage economic story of the Bible as outlined in 5.1 above? Simply by detecting, from Book to Book, the particular unit of *social* or *economic measurement* which the Bible either spoke for or spoke against over the stretches of biblical time. For every socio-political and economic organization in time and space bears the particular signature of the particular unit of social or economic measurement that holds it together and energises it; *Egom, 2004, pp 2-3.* This unit of social or economic measurement may be *labour time* or *public sector debt money* or *private sector commodity money.* So, any meaningful stage theory of economic distribution and human development on this earth must show how the global economy moves from being held together and energised by this one unit of social or economic measurement over this period of time, to being held together and energised by this other unit of social or economic measurement, over this other period of time. In effect, it is the successive units of social or economic measurement which undergird and energise the global economy that tell the running story of when, how and why the global economy has moved from the one stage of economic distribution and human development to the other. Accordingly, the methodology of this economic exegesis of the Bible can be summarized as follows: the labour theory of value is to the barter-exchange communalism of *Genesis to Ruth,* what the public sector debt theory of value is to the money-exchange capitalism of *1 Samuel through Malachi to 2 Maccabees* and the private sector commodity theory of value is to the money-exchange communitarianism of *Matthew to Revelation / Apocalypse.* It is on the basis of these changing social and economic metrics that one can conclusively state that there are three stages in the prophetic and evolutionary economic programme of the Bible as follows; *Egom, 2007a, pp. 53-111.*

5.3.1   The first leg of the Bible's journey to the economic Kingdom of God on this earth, as laid out in the *Books of Genesis to Ruth,* is the somnolent, villagized, barter, mixed-farming, tribal and communalist world of stationary production where one reaps strictly as one sows. Here, *labour-time* is the unit of social measurement and the binding ethic of socio-political and economic life is the tit-for-tat *law of reciprocity* or *lex talionis* and this creates *stationary symmetry* in the distribution of economic opportunities between and among men and nations as *people* and *nations* simply *work for themselves.*

5.3.2   Then the second leg is the boisterous, public-sector-led, urbanised, resource-exporting and resource-importing monetary world of capitalism and extended reproduction as laid out in the *Books of 1 Samuel through Malachi to 2 Maccabees.* Here, the unit of economic measurement is the *public sector debt money* and the binding ethic of socio-economic and political life is the *ceaseless-taking* of the *fiscalist and imperial law of usury and capitalism* which creates and sustains *minor, major to maximum asymmetry* in the distribution of economic opportunities between and among people and nations since people and nations have begun to work for the *bad master* variant of money. It is this *ceaseless-taking law of usury and capitalism* that is already setting up the global economy for implosion through the excessive issuance of the public sector *money of inflation* in the financial convertible and reserve currency nations of the West.

5.3.3   And, finally, the third leg is the restorative, private-sector-led, ambling, villagised and resource-conserving monetary world of communitarianism and extended reproduction as described in the Books of *Matthew to Revelation/Apocalpse.* Here the unit of economic measurement is the *private sector commodity money* and the binding ethic of socio-political and economic life is the *ceaseless-giving of the monetarist law of charity and communitarianism.* This distributive law of God creates and sustains *symmetry and justice* in the distribution of the economic opportunities of jobs, goods and services between and among persons and nations in the global economy since the *good servant* variant of money has begun to work for people and nations.

5.4   Section 2, *Anatomy of Money,* of the *Theory section* of this booklet as above, tells us two things about economic theory.   *One* is that fiscalism is the economic theory and practice of public sector debt money in society which has the habit of turning the public gold of the seed, working and growth capital patrimony of all into the private property and private capital of the few and that the ensuing asymmetry in the distribution of access to financial capital in any society prevents it from producing its members, national and global, into the justice and peace of social and material plenty.   *And, two* is that monetarism is the economic theory and practice of private sector commodity money in society which turns the private capital and private property of the few into the common good capital and patrimony of all so that any society, national or global, is thereby enabled to produce its members into the justice and peace of social and material plenty. Then Section 3, *Economics is Central Banking,* of the same *Theory section* of this booklet as above, tells us that the economic theory and practice of money of any sort is the theory and practice of central banking in society. So, the main point which the economic story of the Bible makes is that the past, present and future ways of money in the global economy mirror the unfolding succession of two central banking traditions: *the usury central banking ethic of Mammon,* on the one hand, and *the charity central banking ethic of God,* on the other hand. Thus, the Bible's evolutionary and prophetic story about the past, present and future ways of money in the global economy falls into two dichotomous central banking traditions as follows.

5.4.1   The first central banking tradition is the story of how public sector *money of inflation* has been pushing the past and current global economy of usury and capitalism into inevitable implosion and financial meltdown. Here, we see how the usury money of Mammon has over the centuries divided the world of trading and paying nations into two unequal groups. The one group consists of the few financial convertible currency and resource-importing nations of the West and the other group comprises the many non-convertible currency and resource-exporting nations of Latin America, Asia and Africa. Because the currencies of the nations of the West are the imperial instruments for facilitating international trade and payments flows and because public sector *money of inflation* is the locomotive of capitalism and imperialism, we note that the nations of the West must continue to inflate their currencies in order to be able to consume goods and services from everywhere on earth without having to pay for these with their own real goods and services, but only in their increasingly valueless public sector debt monies. And the more the nations of the West inflate their currencies in order to control what is produced, how and for whom in all the other nations of the globe, the more the *fiscally unprotected* non-convertible currency and resource exporting nations of the globe are excluded from and marginalized in the global flow of economic life and the more the global economy is being run aground by public sector *money of inflation* precisely as happened in Pharaoh's Egypt, *Genesis 47:13-26,* as follows

Genesis 47:14-15 rings the uncanny but all too familiar bell of *market failure* that one observes in the Nigerian economy, as well as in the global economy, of yesterday and today. For in both latter-day market settings, the seed, working and growth capital patrimony of the many has been so mis-appropriated into the private property and private capital of the few that most Nigerians and most other peoples of the globe have become economically disenfranchised and, therefore, excluded from the Nigerian and global market loops of effective demand as, thus, aptly described in *Genesis 47:15, "Our money is all gone"*. And when the purchasing power of most people has vamoosed into the thin air, then society must find itself in the convulsive grip of the *Argentinean Syndrome* which simply tells us why, how and when a money economy implodes under the weight of public sector *money of inflation*. So, one posits that, in the global economy of the Egypt and the Canaan of yore, the famine was as much an cological disaster which arose from climate change as it was a financial in eltdown that came on the heels of the excessive issuance of public sector debt money by the high and mighty few in society and that this gave rise to the market collapse and financial meltdown of the then money-economy into the barter economy of *Genesis 47:16-19*. And when the barter economy also failed, as is the endemic habit with barter economies, then *Genesis 47:20* tells us that the divine financial insights of Joseph led to the turning of the private capital and private property of the few overlords of   Egyptian society into the common good capital patrimony of all Egyptians when *"all the land became the king's property"*.

5.4.2   But before we go into the specific details of what Joseph did of Trinitarian economic policy in Pharaoh's Egypt to revive and reflate the Egyptian economy of yore, let us look at the second central banking tradition of the prophetic and evolutionary economic story of the Bible. In so doing, we get to appreciate how meticulously consistent the divine economic programme of God is in this our world of Chronos. For, the gist of the economic story of the New Testament from *Matthew to Revelation / Apocalypse* is that after, *or hopefully before,* the entropic market implosion of the current global economy of usury central banking, *an international Exodus banking innovation* will be established in the financial convertible currency nations of the West to engender the orderly and reversed flow of medium to long term capital from the West to the non-convertible currency economies of the rest of the world. In this way, this Exodus banking innovation will emulate Joseph to transform the private capital and private property of the few in the nations of the West into the common good capital and patrimony of all in all the nations of the globe and this is all in line with what St. Paul enjoins us to do in *2 Corinthians 8:13-15.* So, it is only after, *or hopefully before,* the current usury central banking world of capitalism has gone up in the smoke of money inflation, which is already welling up from the monetary bowels of the imperial West, that the new charity central banking world of communitarianism will emerge to make a reserve currency and a resource-conserving State of every trading and paying nation of the globe. This is what the concept of the economic Kingdom of God on earth is really all about. And how, then, did Joseph manage to revive and reflate the economy of Old Egypt in accordance with the *Economic Mind of God?* As follows.

Joseph used the nation-wide network of back-to back stock and commodity exchanges of *Genesis 41:48-49* to transform the *private capital* of the seed and working capital of *corn* and the growth capital of *land* that the hitherto few Egyptian overlords kept and used for themselves into the *common good capital* and patrimony of the seed and working capital of *corn* and the growth capital of *land* which the King now *held in trust* for the use-rights of all Egyptians living and of all Egyptians yet unborn. This is how every Egyptian agro-allied entrepreneur could now access the growth capital of *land* and the seed and working capital of *corn* to venture into the one or the other agribusiness and, in return, he had to pay the stipulated 20% of his annual produce as the *yield on the communitarian investment* of the seed and working capital of *corn* and the growth capital of *land* which the King had made in his agri-business; *Genesis 47:24, 26.* This was the pioneering example of *common good equity financing* at its most elementary and basic form where the Pharaoh, as King, shared in the risk and in the reward of every Egyptian agri-business. So, *Genesis 47:13-26* gives us the rare and summary insight into the nuts and bolts of Biblical Joseph's charity central banking ethic and practice by telling us that any economy of any size grows in local content and in entrepreneurship only when it applies the *Balance Criterion/Rule* of financial market development and management which St. Paul's *2 Corinthians 8:13-15* prescribes for transforming the short-fused stock of the private capital of the few into the medium-long-fused common good capital of all.

And the international mechanism for transforming the unequal capital of the few into the equal capital of all in the global, as in the national, economic setting is the *Exodus banking innovation* which is laid out in *Fig 2* below and is clearly anticipated in *Exodus 11:2-3, 12:35-36*

5.4.3   In fact, *Genesis 47:13-26* captures, in a very graphic manner, the past, present and future of the global economy that is managed after the *Economic Mind of God* as follows: First, the current global economy of usury and capitalism will go up in the smoke of money inflation that is being incubated with the *bad master* variant of money in the imperial nations of the West as in *Fig 1* below. Second, when this happens the global economy will revert to the primitive barter stage where the public sector debt monies of the West will be of no use anymore to anyone for mediating any economic exchanges anywhere in the world. And third, the Economic *Governors of God, EGGs, Genesis 41:37-57,* who are some sort of *spiritual clones* of the Biblical Joseph, will emerge to use the *good servant* variant of money and its Exodus banking innovation of *Fig 2* below to canalize and reticulate short, medium and long term capital from the West to the other nations of the world and to ensure, in the process, that the global economy is restored, reflated and begins to grow the local content of jobs, goods and services equally and abundantly in every nation of the globe. How, then, will this Exodus banking innovation of the good servant variant of money work at the global level, in the continent of Africa and

finally in Nigeria? These are the practical issues of
the *Economic Mind of God* that are briefly addressed in
the rest of this *Practice section* of this booklet; *Egom,
2007a, passim.*

6. Financial Collapse and Rehabilitation of the Globe

6.1   Every capitalist economy of the globe today,
developed and developing, uses public sector debt
money, the *bad master* variant of money, to drive its
economic policy. And, as a result, the twin fiscalist
phenomena of Public Sector Borrowing
Requirement, PSBR, and Interest, emerge in every
capitalist economy of yesterday and today to bring
about asymmetry in the distribution of the economic
opportunities of jobs, goods and services among and
between persons of gender, creed and race, at home
and abroad. *Egom 2006, pp 27-60.*

6.2   For as soon as the twin fiscalist phenomena of PSBR
and Interest emerge in any public-sector-driven and
demand-led economy, so is a gap of resource-
unemployment and industrial outsourcing
interposed between its money supply market
structure, or its financial circulation of money, and
its money demand and use market structure, or its
industrial circulation of money. The result of this is
that the *public gold* of the seed, working and growth
capital patrimony of all in society is gradually but
irreversibly transformed, through various corrupt
and corrupting forms of induced and contrived
market imperfection, into the *private property* and

private gold of the few in society. This is the self-immolating way of the social ethic of usury and capitalism in the global society.

6.3   It is the twin fiscalist phenomena of PSBR and Interest which continue to divide the global economy into the first-tier of the few reserve and financial convertible currency nations of the West, on the one hand, and the second-tier of the many non-reserve and non-convertible currency nations of the global South and Eastern Europe, on the other hand. And, as a result of this, the public gold of the seed, working and growth capital patrimony of the many non-reserve and non-convertible currency nations of the globe is always transformed, in the form of non-gold international reserves, into the private gold of the few reserve and financial convertible currency nations of the West. This is what it means to say that the reserve currency nations of the West borrow the liquidity of non-gold international reserves from the non-reserve currency nations of the globe, so that, quite surprisingly and in conformity with the novel central banking insight of the Italian economist, Marcello de Cecco: *de Cecco 1984, passim,* the latter are always the central bankers to the former. It, therefore, insults the intelligence of reasonable people when the reserve currency nations of the West do pretend to be the donors of this and of that to the non-convertible currency nations of the globe when it is clearly the latter who are the all-round and thankless donors of reserve currency surpluses to the West.

6.4   As the public gold of the second-tier and non-reserve currency nations of the globe is being exported and accumulated, as non-gold international reserves, in the central banking domains of the reserve currency nations of the West, we find that the money supply market structures of the former, in line with the perceptive observations of Professor Robert Triffin in the Latin American economies of the 1940s: *Triffin, 1966, passim,* are exported to and ensconced within the central banking domains of the latter. It is this yawning and colonising gap of resource unemployment and industrial outsourcing, which peripheral capitalism interposes, in consequence, between the exported money supply market structures and the home-bound, *but decapitated,* money demand and use market structures of these second-tier nations of the globe, that is responsible for their resilient economic backwardness. In other words, it is the twin fiscalist phenomena of PSBR and Interest which starve and deprive the peoples of the second-tier and non-convertible currency nations of the globe of their seed, working and growth capital patrimonies for their integral human development. Consequently, these economies will not grow in home-made goods, jobs and services unless and until their international reserves are repatriated, kept and managed at home and in gold to support and underwrite the deepening of their domestic capital and commodity markets.

6.5   Notice in Fig. 1 below that the twin fiscalist phenomena of PSBR and Interest have continued

**Fig 1. Global Private Gold: Non-Gold International Reserves
1968 - 2006**

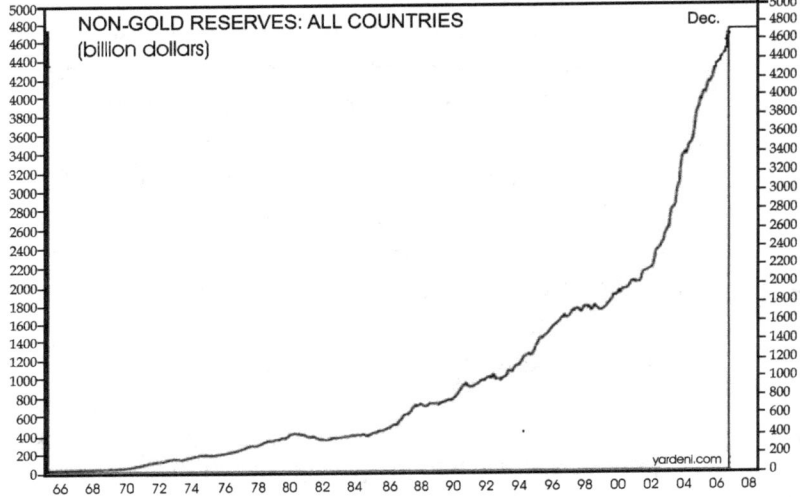

since 1968 to sustain a yearly astronomical rise in the volume of global non-gold international reserves. In 1973, it stood at 300 billion US Dollars but, in December 2006, it had escalated to 4.75 trillion US Dollars and, of this amount, over 3.35 trillion US Dollars came from the developing world. Accordingly, an increasingly yawning and *self-colonising* gap of resource unemployment and industrial outsourcing has emerged since 1968 between the money supply market structures and the money demand and use market structures of the very first-tier nations of the West. So, in spite of the very rosy newswire statistics that one reads and hears everyday about the economies of the West, the fact remains that their financial and industrial fundamentals do say the stark contrary that there is economic distress in the first-tier nations of the West on account of the spiral of money inflation there.

For, whenever and wherever the twin fiscalist phenomena of the PSBR and Interest are actively at work, there and then must one expect money inflation spiral to lead an economy to decay interminably in home-made goods, jobs and services. So, any variant of the now standard *inflation targeting* monetary policy in any capitalist economy is the true nature of the usury central banking method and process of transforming the public gold of all into the private gold of the few and thereby inducing loss of local content in any capitalist economy. Indeed, non-gold international reserves increase by leaps and bounds in the central banking domains of the first-tier nations of the West only because their PSBRs increase by leaps and bounds as their levels of local content must correspondingly fall in leaps and bounds.

6.6   The astronomical growth since 1968 in global non-gold international reserves in the central banking domains of the West has had no outlets for productive investments in the West and it is not being drained or reticulated to the second-tier nations of Africa and elsewhere for that purpose either. So, sooner than later, the money inflation pressure that is thus bottled up in the central banking domains of the West will engender the total collapse of the global economy in much the same way as money inflation imploded Argentina in 2001.

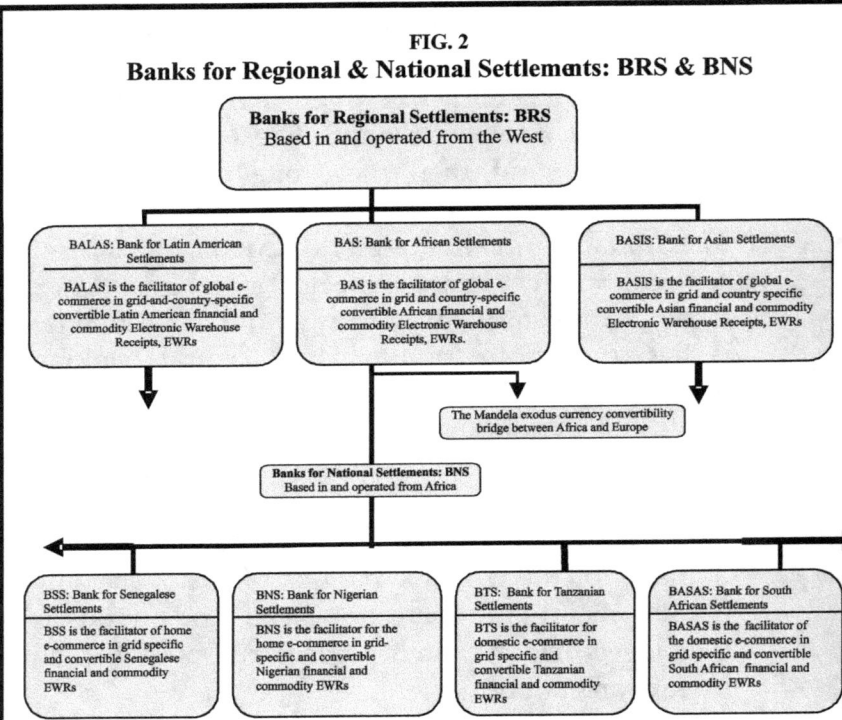

FIG. 2
Banks for Regional & National Settlements: BRS & BNS

Banks for Regional Settlements: BRS
Based in and operated from the West

BALAS: Bank for Latin American Settlements

BALAS is the facilitator of global e-commerce in grid-and-country-specific convertible Latin American financial and commodity Electronic Warehouse Receipts, EWRs

BAS: Bank for African Settlements

BAS is the facilitator of global e-commerce in grid and country-specific convertible African financial and commodity Electronic Warehouse Receipts, EWRs.

BASIS: Bank for Asian Settlements

BASIS is the facilitator of global e-commerce in grid and country specific convertible Asian financial and commodity Electronic Warehouse Receipts, EWRs

The Mandela exodus currency convertibility bridge between Africa and Europe

Banks for National Settlements: BNS
Based in and operated from Africa

BSS: Bank for Senegalese Settlements

BSS is the facilitator of home e-commerce in grid specific and convertible Senegalese financial and commodity EWRs

BNS: Bank for Nigerian Settlements

BNS is the facilitator for the home e-commerce in grid-specific and convertible Nigerian financial and commodity EWRs

BTS: Bank for Tanzanian Settlements

BTS is the facilitator for domestic e-commerce in grid specific and convertible Tanzanian financial and commodity EWRs

BASAS: Bank for South African Settlements

BASAS is the facilitator of the domestic e-commerce in grid specific and convertible South African financial and commodity EWRs

The Mandela currency convertibility bridge between the Europe-based BAS and the Africa-based BNS, eliminates, within the BAS global electronic market network for e-commerce in convertible grid- and country-specific financial and commodity EWRs of the non-reserve currency nations of Africa, the existing and asymmetric currency non-convertibility gulf between Europe and Africa through the restorative reticulation of surplus capital from Europe to Africa. The Mandela is the gold-convertible African common currency which has the virtual unit value of 29 grams of fine gold just like the defunct gold franc of the Bank for International Settlements, BIS, of Basle, Switzerland.

6.7   Thus, the road to social and material plenty for all in the global economy is paved with interest-free private sector commodity money, the *good servant* variant of money, whilst the road to social and material want for the most in the global economy is paved with interest-based public sector debt money, the *bad master* variant of money. How, then, can and will the global economy transit from the poverty-inducing regime of usury central banking to the wealth-creating dispensation of charity central banking? This can and will be smoothly brought about via the Exodus banking innovation and ramp of *Banks for Regional and National Settlements, BRS & BNS,* as shown in Fig 2 above. BRS and BNS are, respectively, the international and national banking institutions which essentially drain and reticulate medium-to-long term capital from surplus areas to deficit areas, globally and nationally, and, thereby, create balanced growth and development for all and sundry in time and space after the *Economic Mind of God* and as enjoined on us by St. Paul in *2 Corinthians 8:13-15.* Indeed, BRS and BNS are the *Exodus banking visible hands* which the world will begin to use quite soon to make citizens all and subjects none of all human beings in time and space.

7.   BAS: Bank for African Settlements

7.1   With the collapse of the US Dollar based *fixed-rate gold exchange debt standard* in December 1958 and with the swamping of the world, from the 1960s, with the increasingly goldless and valueless reserve currencies of the West, and especially the US Dollar, the ensuing and colonising phenomenon of industrial outsourcing began to destroy the old industrial bases of the first-tier nations of the West and, naturally, of course, the infant and post-colonial industrial bases of the second-tier nations of Sub-Saharan Africa. This is how a new three-legged pattern has emerged, since the 1970s, in the international division of industrial labour among the nations of the globe. Accordingly, the first-tier nations of the West are now mainly into the casino capitalism of the global services/tertiary sector, the second-tier but newly industrialising nations of the East, mainly, have taken over the industrial capitalism of the global secondary / manufacturing sector and the second-tier but low-local-content-growing Sub-Saharan African nations, especially, are still trapped in the outsourcing and peripheral capitalism of the global primary/extractive sector. Sub-Saharan Africa is, as it were, the eternal resource reservoir or warehouse of the global economy.

Such a global economy which has continued to encourage the nations of the rest of the world, over the centuries, to take their imperial turns at pillaging the resources of Africa, in total disregard of the wishes of the Africans themselves, bears the characteristic signature and banner of the usury central banking ethic and practice of Mammon. Consequently, the new global economy of justice and peace will emerge as soon as Africa is insulated from any *predatory bouts of pillage and scramble* from any

nation of the global South and of the global North as
well. And this is what the charity central banking
ethic and practice of God is poised to do with Africa
and with the whole world quite soon. Hence, Africa,
the current sick and weak man of the global
economy, is, indeed, the Achilles heel of the current
global economy of usury and capitalism and, quite
naturally, Africa is and will remain the inevitable
open sesame for the re-emergence of God's Garden of
Eden on this earth! After all, and as Pliny the Elder is
said to have remarked long ago, *something new always
comes out of Africa* - **Ex Africa semper aliquid novum.**

7.2   So, the current three-legged global economic order of
usury and capitalism is irreversibly on the wane.
For, if the Fifth WTO Ministerial at Cancun, Mexico,
September 10-14 2003, is anything to go by, then this
new three-legged pattern in the international
division of labour among the nations of the globe is
the halfway house of a very incomplete work in
progress. Why so? Because, as Fig 1 and Section 6 of
this booklet have indicated above, the global
capitalist economic order is being done to death by
the excessive accumulation of non-gold international
reserves in the central banking domains of the first-
tier nations of the West. And as the current global
capitalist economy of the floating rate regime of
usury central banking is going up in the smoke of
money inflation, the new global communitarian
economic order of justice and peace will be
overtaking the world. At the centre of this emerging
fixed rate global gold commodity standard is the

global exodus banking innovation of BAS: *Bank for African Settlements,* which will weave Homeland Africa and the Diaspora African nations of Europe and the Americas into a dynamic web of balanced growth in the local contents of jobs, goods and services.

7.3   Indeed, a co-prosperity economic zone has become an urgent necessity for the West and for Africa for two reasons. One, the interminable and diabolical Structural Adjustment Programmes of the IMF and the World Bank that have come to Africa , since the 1970s, have laid waste the embryonic and import-substituting manufacturing bases of Africa. And, two, the money inflation spiral of non-gold international reserves that has come to the West, see Fig. 1 above, since the 1970s,has forced Europe and North America to increasingly outsource their industrial production to the newly industrialising economies of India, Brazil and especially China. This has led to Africa becoming, from the 1970s, the captive markets for China's industrial products, since Europe and North America have already become, through their industrial outsourcing policy to the *slave-wage areas* of the world, the captive markets for China's industrial products as well. But this is not in the home economic interests of Africa or of the Diaspora-African nations of Europe and North America either. So what to do? Africa and Europe need to use, in equal partnership, the NEPAD initiative, *www.nepad.org,* to devise and build a deep and resilient monetary and financial bridge between their respective webs of currency, financial and industrial markets and to use this *Mandela convertible currency bridge* as the corridor for developing the exclusive Euro-African co-prosperity market zone of balanced growth in home-made goods, jobs and services. It is *BAS: Bank for African Settlements,* that enables Europe and Africa to do so. For BAS will drain and reticulate excess seed, working and growth capital of non-gold international reserves from Europe to Africa to support and underwrite the deepening of Africa's capital and commodity markets for Africa's sustainable growth in local content and for the derivative growth in Europe's investment income from, and industrial markets in, Africa.

7.4   What BAS is really equipped to do is to transit any African economy from the asymmetry in economic distribution, which goes with the economic policy territory of public sector debt money, to the symmetry in economic distribution, which emerges when an African economy uses private sector commodity money to drive its economic policy. This BAS does by using the interest-free and risk-ready *Mandela private sector commodity money, the emerging gold convertible African common currency,* to support and underwrite the deepening of the capital and commodity markets of the pan-African economy. BAS is, thus, the win-win market development and banking initiative which, under the current floating rate and global two-tier structure of reserve and non-reserve currencies, will steadily grow local content in the reserve currency nations of Europe and North America as well as in the regional pocket of the currently non-reserve, but emerging reserve, currency nations of the African continent.

7.5 BAS is the modern-day version of what the Peréire brothers, Isaac and Emile, of 19th century France called *crédit mobilier*, which they used to carry out great undertakings of infrastructural development in the France, Switzerland, Spain and Russia of that century, *www.jewishencyclopedia.com*. Thus BAS, like *crédit mobilier*, is on the market scene of Africa to develop and manage development corridors of deep capital and commodity markets and the accompanying land, air and sea support corridors that would not only bring sustainable growth in local content to this beleaguered cradle of human civilization but would also take development to the very door-steps of the African in his rural and cultural surroundings. BAS is, therefore, synonymous with an African industrial location policy which will bring about a permanent reversal in the current post-colonial and massive rural-urban drift of Africans in the working age bracket of 20-65 years. And, so, BAS will use the market mechanism to decongest the urban and sprawling ghettoes of Africa's unkempt mega-cities like Dakar, Nairobi, Lagos, Kinshasa, Johannesburg etc., and ruralise Africa's working population in aid of agro-allied growth in local content all over the continent. The market content of such an industrial location policy of balanced population spread all over the continent of Africa is the continent-wide ICT network of back-to-back stock and commodity exchanges which is the electronic heart and backbone of the BAS economic agenda for a renascent Africa .

7.6   Registered and headquartered in a strategic reserve currency nation of Europe, BAS has the two-fold task of:

•   *Building and operating the global risk-averting and risk-controlling electronic market infrastructure for international trade and payments in convertible African capital and commodity market instruments.*

!   *Attracting and encouraging, with the aid of appropriate and convertible financial and commodity market instruments, the steady inflow of risk-ready reserve currency funds into the emerging reserve currency capital and commodity markets of Africa.*

BAS performs this two-fold task of capital and commodity market development in the emerging reserve currency nations of Africa in three steps as follows:

•   *Develops and manages the electronic market networks for on-line trade in the grid and country-specific financial and commodity Electronic Warehouse Receipts, EWRs, of the emerging reserve currency nations of Africa.*

•   *Facilitates the on-line trade in the grid-and country-specific financial and commodity EWRs of the emerging reserve currency nations of Africa.*

- *Trains and partners with up-and-coming African entrepreneurs to establish and operate national clusters of specialized warehousing and electronic marketing sites for on-line trade in grid-and-country-specific financial and commodity EWRs of the emerging reserve currency nations of Africa.*

8.   Financial Rehabilitation of Nigeria

8.1   The Nigerian economy is a big house of an African market place where, today, some 140 million souls trade jobs, goods and services for the naira, the Nigerian currency of trade and payments. And, the roof or the canopy of this big house of an African market place is the Nigerian monetary system. It is here that the Central Bank of Nigeria, CBN, manages, through the activities of 25 jumbo Nigerian commercial banks, the use of the naira by Nigerians to trade jobs, goods and services. When the CBN does its job well through its directorates for the Nigerian currency, financial and commodity markets, Nigerians grow, across the land, in social and material plenty. But, when the CBN does a hash of its job, as has been its wont for the past two decades of its astigmatic and retrogressive economic reforms in Nigeria, Nigerians must continue to bear the increasing social and material burdens of monetary mismanagement. For these days, Nigerians trade little of home-made goods, jobs and services with the naira among themselves because the Nigerian monetary canopy has a short-term-view and does, as

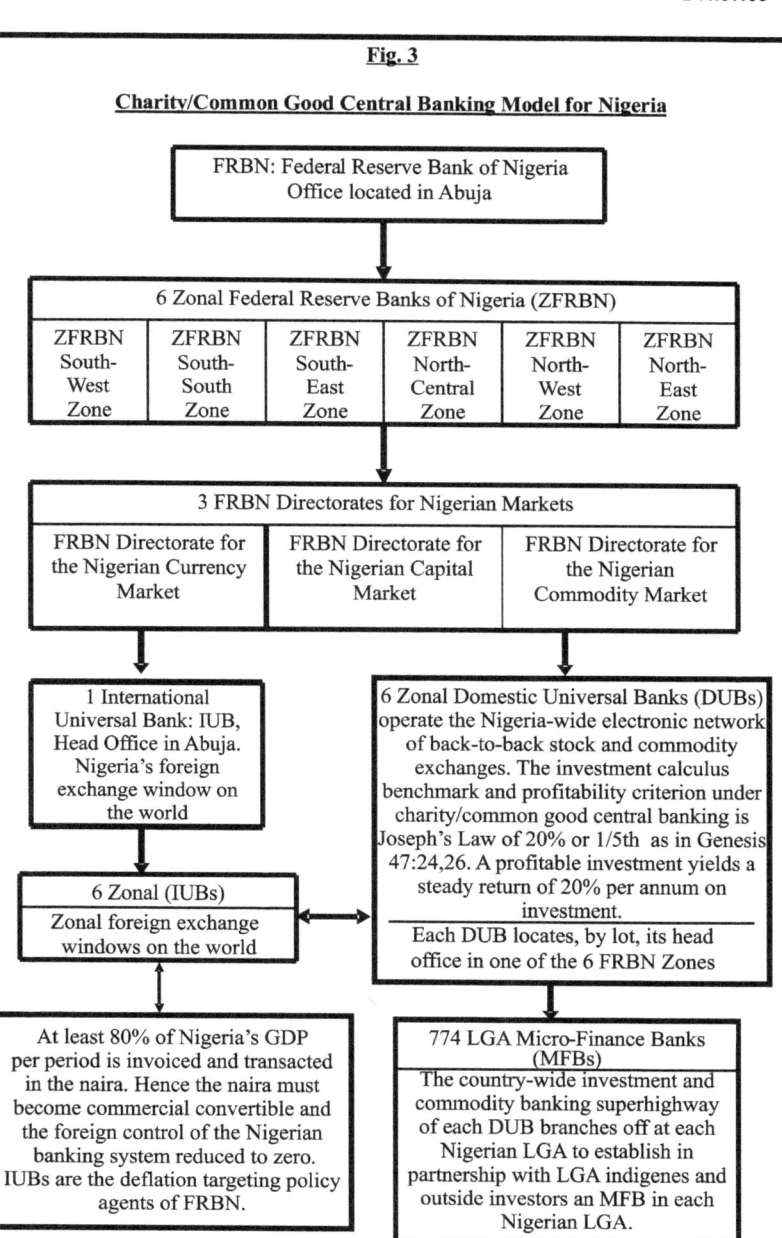

Fig. 3

Charity/Common Good Central Banking Model for Nigeria

FRBN: Federal Reserve Bank of Nigeria
Office located in Abuja

6 Zonal Federal Reserve Banks of Nigeria (ZFRBN)

ZFRBN South-West Zone	ZFRBN South-South Zone	ZFRBN South-East Zone	ZFRBN North-Central Zone	ZFRBN North-West Zone	ZFRBN North-East Zone

3 FRBN Directorates for Nigerian Markets

FRBN Directorate for the Nigerian Currency Market	FRBN Directorate for the Nigerian Capital Market	FRBN Directorate for the Nigerian Commodity Market

1 International Universal Bank: IUB, Head Office in Abuja. Nigeria's foreign exchange window on the world

6 Zonal Domestic Universal Banks (DUBs) operate the Nigeria-wide electronic network of back-to-back stock and commodity exchanges. The investment calculus benchmark and profitability criterion under charity/common good central banking is Joseph's Law of 20% or 1/5th as in Genesis 47:24,26. A profitable investment yields a steady return of 20% per annum on investment.

Each DUB locates, by lot, its head office in one of the 6 FRBN Zones

6 Zonal (IUBs)
Zonal foreign exchange windows on the world

At least 80% of Nigeria's GDP per period is invoiced and transacted in the naira. Hence the naira must become commercial convertible and the foreign control of the Nigerian banking system reduced to zero. IUBs are the deflation targeting policy agents of FRBN.

774 LGA Micro-Finance Banks (MFBs)
The country-wide investment and commodity banking superhighway of each DUB branches off at each Nigerian LGA to establish in partnership with LGA indigenes and outside investors an MFB in each Nigerian LGA.

a result, shy away from the rural landmass and rural dwellers of Nigeria. This is so because the CBN manages Nigeria's international reserves outside of Nigeria. And, by thus putting the centre of gravity of the Nigerian monetary canopy outside of Nigeria, the naira is condemned into being and remaining a public-sector-led, consumption-prone, work-shy, rural-shy and non-convertible currency that is being done steadily to death by imported inflation as Professor Triffin foretold in the 1940s.

8.2 Unfortunately, Nigeria does not follow China and India to pursue such stringent exchange control rules that would enable the non-convertible naira to become production-prone, rural-friendly and to thus, engender the growth of local content in Nigeria. But all hope is not lost in this regard. For there is a market-oriented alternative to what China and India do of rigorous exchange control in aid of their balanced growth in local content. This market-oriented alternative to stringent exchange control laws requires the CBN to manage Nigeria's international reserves in gold within the central banking domain of Nigeria. And the most important first step in this direction is the consolidation and phased liquidation of Nigeria's domestic public sector debt stock. For,it is through the total elimination of the Nigerian PSBR that the interest phenomenon will disappear from Nigeria. This is what *deflation-targeting* monetary policy is all about; *Egom 2006, pp 57-58, 195, 224-228.* And, as soon as deflation targeting monetary policy makes the twin fiscalist phenomena of PSBR and Interest to disappear from the Nigerian market structure of money supply, the *centre of gravity* of the Nigerian monetary canopy is as good as already in Nigeria. For money supply management in Nigeria will cease, on this account, to be *exogenously-induced* through the Nigerian public sector for the benefit of the Nigerian public sector, but will become *endogenously-driven* by the Nigerian private sector for the benefit of the Nigerian private sector. *Thus, managing the naira for the common good begins with the elimination of public sector debt naira from the Nigerian currency market; Egom 2004, pp. 175-182*

It is this that will make the naira a work-happy, a rural-friendly, a resource-conserving, an international and a commercial convertible currency. And in the wake of this, the Nigerian monetary canopy will take on the medium-long-term view, become production-prone all over the rural landmass of Nigeria and, inexorably, will lead Nigerians to use the naira to trade jobs, goods and services aplenty among themselves. This is the métier of the charity central banking ethic and practice of God as laid out in Fig. 3 above. It situates the locus of banking reform in Nigeria within the *privatisation and internalisation of control* over the money creation and distribution process in the Nigerian currency market. This deflation-targeting monetary policy contrasts markedly with the current practice of banking reform in Nigeria where *inflation targeting* monetary policy entrenches the more the *fiscalisation and externalisation of control* over the money creation and distribution process in the Nigerian currency market. Whereas the latter is monetary policy after the usury and avaricious economic mind of Mammon, which saddles Nigeria with a *fragile* monetary canopy of the short-term view, the former is monetary policy after the charity and sacrificial Economic Mind of God, which readily equips Nigeria with the *robust* monetary canopy of the medium-long-term view.

For what happens when the Nigerian monetary canopy takes on the medium-long-term view and becomes robust, work-happy and production-prone across the length and breadth of Nigeria is that *gung-ho* and ambulant Nigerian investment and commodity banking establishments arise everywhere to mobilize every enterprising Nigerian to use the naira to trade jobs, goods and services with other Nigerians without having to shift his base of business operations from his village or LGA. Development is, as it were, brought to his very door-steps in his native rural and cultural surroundings by what the Peréire brothers (Isaac and Emile) of 19th century France called *crédit mobilier*. And this is precisely what the balanced growth of *resource control* means and entails for the Nigerian. He is enabled by the country-wide Nigerian network of ambulant investment and commodity banks to get reasonably well-off in social and material circumstances by trading his local resources of jobs, goods and services for the naira from his own rural catchment area. It is such an industrial location policy that will bring about a permanent reversal to the massive rural-urban drift of Nigeria's population. And, if the truth be told, Nigeria cannot grow in social and material plenty unless economic policy reform uses the market mechanism to decongest Lagos and other Nigerian urban centres and to ruralise Nigeria's population. The market content of such an industrial location policy of balanced population spread all over Nigeria is the nationwide electronic network of back-to-back stock and commodity exchanges of Fig 3 above.

8.3   However, the Nigerian monetary canopy cannot take on the medium to long-term view and become, robust, work-happy and production-prone across Nigeria unless the CBN changes its current mind-set about where the centre of gravity of the Nigerian monetary system should be located. For, right from 1914 to this very day, the centre of gravity of the Nigerian monetary system has continued to be located in the central banking domains of the nations of the West. It is understandable that Nigeria, during the colonial period of 1914 -1960, had to keep and manage her international reserves within the imperial financial system of Britain. In this way, Britain expropriated Nigeria's savings, *the very bedrock of the Nigerian monetary system*, for her imperial use around the globe. This is what happens to any colony. But, Nigeria ceased to be a colony 46 years ago! Why should the nations of the West continue to expropriate Nigeria's savings for their imperial use at home and abroad and all of this to the social and material discomfort of the Nigerian?

There is no justifiable economic reason for politically independent Nigeria to persist in keeping and managing her international reserves in the central banking domains of the West. The colonial argument that Nigeria's international reserves should be kept abroad to cover at least six months of Nigeria's average import bill is a very lame one and only goes to say that the naira is a public-sector-led, local and non-convertible currency. It does not in any way explain why the naira should not become a private-sector-led, a reserve, a resource conserving, an international and a commercial convertible currency. And, why, indeed, should Nigeria not produce at home much of what she imports from abroad? How else can Nigeria create job security for Nigerians in Nigeria if not through endogenous increases in local content?

8.4   What is certain is that Nigeria has been trapped for the past four-plus decades in the monetary quandary of *ethical mis-direction*. The CBN says that Nigeria will grow in local content as some ten or less jumbo commercial banks of Nigeria become the junior partners of some imperial commercial banking houses of the West in managing Nigeria's international reserves in the central banking domains of the West. But this cannot be so for this particular regimen of international reserves management goes against the grain of the charity central banking ethic and practice of God! In fact, the

Economic Mind of God says that Nigeria's commercial/universal banks have the primary job to manage the use of naira funds to grow local content in Nigeria as mapped out in Fig 3. above. They should be *great local players* by taking short, medium and long-term naira funds to grow, and expand the scope of, rural businesses in Nigeria in the communitarian spirit of *Genesis 47:23-24.*

But, contrarily, the public-sector-led and interest-based currency market policy which Nigeria has pursued, especially from September 26, 1986 to this very day, devalues the naira *sine-die* through the dishonest, avaricious, unpatriotic, diabolical and colonial taxation policy of removing cooked-up and phantom subsidies from the pump-prices of basic fuel commodities, keeps the Nigerian level of interest rates in the sky through the treasonous and fiscalist monetary policy of forex round-tripping, gives a short-fuse to the naira and makes naira funds to have a deep rural aversion. In fact, the rabid *inflation-targeting* banking reform that has been on-going in Nigeria since 2003 cannot but have the very unpatriotic objective of returning Nigeria to the *financial and industrial tabula rasa* of a full-blown colony; *Egom 2006, pp 94-98, 212-220.* Inflation-targeting monetary policy is being used to deprive Nigerians of their patrimony of *public gold* and to *pied-pipe* Nigeria into the *Hamelinian abyss* and financial thraldom of *Deut. 28:43* and *Isaiah 3:12* where foreign and hostile interests from the financial convertible currency West are given full control of

Nigeria's banking system and Nigeria will, then, turn out to be a Gambia or a Liberia! This is why there is today a deluge of foreign investments into the Nigerian banking industry so that tomorrow the few consolidated Nigerian banking houses may become a vampire set of neo-colonial, big-for-nothing, and toothless industrial bulldogs of an African Development Bank, ADB, or of an emergent African Finance Corporation, AFC. The West is, as usual, bent on putting a permanent and colonial gap of industrial outsourcing between the Nigerian naira supply market structure and the Nigerian naira demand and use market structure. *Egom 2004, pp 87-106.* This is the sum-total of the colonial and unpatriotic sense in the much touted, but quite vacuous, economic reforms of the 4th Republic in Nigeria. Quislings all!

However, Figs 1 and 2 above say it quite clearly that this on-going reform of economic treachery and sabotage in Nigeria will assuredly come to naught. In fact, it will explode in the face of the West and of the very sorry pack of their unctuous, and, quite distastefully, subservient Nigerian hirelings; *Isaiah 50:11.*

So, the CBN's major task does not lie with the *quixotic, traitorous, vain and quite colonising idea* of making *global players* of Nigeria's commercial banks but, rather, in making the *naira risk-ready and rural-friendly.* This requires the deepening of Nigeria's markets for savings which, in turn, requires a currency market policy of *naira revaluation*. But the naira cannot be revalued unless Nigeria's international reserves are managed at home and in gold within Nigeria! And, the market framework for managing Nigeria's international reserves at home and in gold is the country-wide electronic network of back-to-back stock and commodity exchanges which the charity central banking ethic and practice of God will, in the very due course, use to gird around Nigeria as per Fig 3. above and in line with *Genesis 41:48-49.*

8.5   Finally, the core money supply management message of Fig 3 above is that the more actively present a Nigerian commercial bank becomes in facilitating the day-to-day economic life of rural Nigeria, the more it is qualified to manage Nigeria's international reserves at *home* and *abroad*. Therefore, the sole criterion which a Nigerian commercial bank must fully satisfy in order to become one of the emerging *big six* of the commercial / universal banks, which are going to be, as per Fig 3 above, the custodians of Nigeria's international reserves at *home* and *abroad,* is that it has physical and active *micro-finance-banking* presence in each of the 774 LGAs of Nigeria. Thus, charity will begin at home but will not remain at home on account of the savings management *balancing work* of BRS and BNS of Fig. 2 above.

Yes, the Nigerian economy has long been mired in *autocratic* social and material distress because it has, over the decades, continued to use public sector debt naira, *the bad master variant of naira,* to drive its economic policy after the avaricious economic mind of Mammon. But, the Nigerian economy of the immediate future will bask in *democratic* social and material plenty because it will use private sector commodity naira, *the good servant variant of naira,* to drive its economic policy after the sacrificial Economic Mind of God.

Conclusion

"Some day there will be a king who rules with integrity, and national leaders who govern with justice. Each of them will be like a shelter from the wind and a place to hide from storms. They will be like streams flowing in the desert, like the shadow of a giant rock in a barren land. Their eyes and ears will be open to the needs of the people. They will not be impatient any longer, but they will act with understanding and will say what they mean" Isaiah: 32:1-4.

9   Crossroads of the World

9.1   Most social scientists and theologians greet with deep scepticism and often with derisive conceit the idea of the *Economic Mind of God* as portrayed above. They simply cannot come to terms with the idea that God is very concerned about how we live and thrive on this earth and that He has His own Trinitarian money supply management programme for the globe. However, the Christians among them do say the Lord's Prayer every so often. And there is the rub! For when they so do, they do ask for the Kingdom of God to come to this earth. And when the Kingdom of God truly and soon does come to this earth, would it not do so with God's Trinitarian money supply management programme in tow? It certainly would. Thus, the Lord's Prayer justifies the above inquiry into the theory and practice of the *Economic Mind of God.*

9.2   The Exodus banking innovation of *Fig 2* above, which is rooted in *Exodus 11:2-3, 12:35-36* and in St. Paul's *Balance Criterion* of *2 Corinthians 8:13-15* for savings management in the financial market of any economy, national or global, is at the core foundation of the *Economic Mind of God* or *Trinitarian Economics.* It is this charity central banking ethic of communitarianism that Biblical Joseph used in Pharaoh's Egypt, *Genesis 41: 48-49; 47: 13-26,* to make citizens all and subjects none of the Egyptians of yore. So the *Economic Mind of God* is at work on this earth when the global and national two-some of the

Exodus banking innovations of BRS and BNS, of Fig. 2 above, combine to give the *financial viability* of food, job and social security to every human being at the *crossroads* of the world as in *Ezekiel 38:12, Judges 18:7, Isaiah 32:15-18*

9.3 So, when will the earth be enveloped in the currency, financial and industrial market glory of God as the waters cover the sea?; *Habakkuk 2:14; Joel 2:24-26.* When and only when the charity central banking ethic and practice of God girds the earth and uses the interest-free and private-sector commodity money to distribute work and its rewards, social and material, evenly among persons of sex, race, and creed within and between all the nations of the globe. For, from this time onwards and onwards, the earth will become, *once again,* God's Garden of Eden which, *once again,* is located at the *crossroads* of Kairos and Chronos, with Africa, *once again,* as its centrepiece! *Marana Tha!.*

> *Be glad, earth and sky*
> *Roar, sea, and every creature in you ;*
> *be glad, fields and everything in you!*
> *The trees in the wood will shout for joy*
> *when the Lord comes to rule the earth.*
> *He will rule the peoples of the world*
> *with justice and fairness.*
> *Psalm 96:11-13*

References

1. Egom, P. A., 1977, *"Money in the Theory of International Economic Activity: An inquiry into the Nature and Causes of the Wealth and Poverty of Nations".*

2. Adione-Egom,L,2002,`Globalization at the Crossroads: Capitalism or Communalism?'*

3. de Cecco; M. 1984 *"Money and Empire: The International Gold Standard".*

4. Egom, P.A.,2004,`NEPAD and the Common Good'*

5. Egom, P.A.,2006,`Compass for Economic Reform'*

6. Egom,P.A.,2007a, `Economics of Justice & Peace'*

7. Triffin R., 1966 *"The World Money Maze: National Currencies in International Payments".*